36 Games Kids Love to Play

ADRIAN HARRISON

WITH ILLUSTRATIONS
BY THE AUTHOR

All net proceeds from the sale of *36 Games Kids Love to Play* support the work of Northeast Foundation for Children, a non-profit, educational organization whose mission is to foster safe, challenging, and joyful classrooms and schools, K–8.

ISBN 1892989069

Library of Congress catalog card number 2001097854

Illustrations: Adrian Harrison

Cover and book design: Woodward Design

Northeast Foundation for Children
39 Montague City Road
Greenfield, MA 01301
1-800-360-6332

www.responsiveclassroom.org

07 06 05 04 03   9 8 7 6 5 4 3 2

DEDICATION

To my Da, Maurice Harrison, the best father one could wish for,
and my Ma, Theresa Harrison, who in the years
since her passing has been with me constantly.

And to Laurie, my friend, teammate, wife, and inspiration.

ACKNOWLEDGEMENTS

This book is the result of collaboration among many people. In particular, I would like to thank the following:

Alice Yang, editor at Northeast Foundation for Children, for her editorial skill, her caring support, and her facilitation of each step of the process. Her thoughtful consideration of both the large picture and the textual details helped me move the book from conception to final manuscript.

Lynn Bechtel, editor at Northeast Foundation for Children, for her help in editing this book as well as her skill and attention to detail in copyediting and proofreading. Her ability to make decisions in a timely yet caring manner ensured that the book moved smoothly through its production stages.

Mary Beth Forton, editorial director of Northeast Foundation for Children, for drawing on both her teaching and editorial experience to fine-tune these games and make the book easy to use. Her wise answers to questions large and small, her warm encouragement, and her ability to see and bring forth the best in everyone made this project a success.

Jay Lord, master teacher and game facilitator, for helping to reflect on and articulate the importance of play and the role of the teacher in conducting games.

Roxann Kriete, executive director of Northeast Foundation for Children, for giving me the opportunity to write this book; for her vision and intelligence; and for knowing when to step back, giving everyone space to do his or her work, and when to roll up her sleeves and help with the nitty-gritties.

Chip Wood for his advice, insights, and time that helped shape the content and direction of this book in its early stages.

Leslie and Jeff Woodward, designers, for creating a book that is at once beautiful, lively, user-friendly, and practical.

Ruth Charney, consulting teacher for Northeast Foundation for Children and author of *Teaching Children to Care,* for her support, guidance, time, and most of all, inspiration.

Bean na ti, women's soccer team, for showing me the benefit of play at every age.

I would also like to thank **my family,** whose names appear in the pages of this book. They say you can't choose your family, but if I could, I would choose each and every one of you. To **Monique, Lena, and Alex,** thank you for being my game guinea pigs. And to **the pupils of Upper Middle 5,** thank you for being my play pals. Finally, to **the teachers I have had the joy of working with at the Greenfield Center School,** thank you for the knowledge you readily pass on.

TABLE OF CONTENTS

iNTRODUCTiON

The importance of play

A few years ago, a small town in western Massachusetts built a new elementary school. As part of the opening celebration, graduates of the old school were invited back to reminisce. Person after person after person—teenager to old-ager—spoke not of the classroom but of the playground. They spoke of the games in general and of specific memories like kicking the ball over the schoolhouse roof into the hands of the other team. They remembered what was most important to them. They remembered play.

It is in our nature to play. We play games to have fun, to build community, and to develop physical skills. Through play we also develop social skills like cooperation, empathy, assertion, and self-control. Well played, games are clique busters because they require us to include everyone in the group, to mix and mingle with people other than our best pals. Well played, games are challenging and fun without being mean. They invoke rule and compromise. They're about winning and losing and losing and winning and learning that it's no big deal either way.

Making space for games in school—indeed, making games an integral part of the curriculum—honors children's development and their need to have fun. The fun of a game can enliven a day, clarify and focus academics, and help all classroom members know and be known to each other.

Playing games also helps us create the playful atmosphere that is so important to children's learning. But simply engaging in a game does not guarantee playfulness. Teachers must model playfulness throughout the day—in games and in many of the routines of the classroom, from greeting children at arrival to sending them off at bus pickup. Playful does not mean silly, mindless, or out of control; it does mean active and flexible, cooperative and caring. It means having a sense of humor and a sense of adventure. We must be playful ourselves if we want our games and our classrooms to be full of play and full of learning. Being playful allows learning at its very best.

Managing games

To play games well takes preparation. Children do not necessarily come to school knowing how to play safely. They do not come to school knowing how to include everyone in fun, rather than just a few. But we can teach them. And this teaching is crucial, for children can release themselves to play only when they trust in the safety of their physical and social environment.

Signals for safety

To maintain safety, we need to teach children a signal or two that mean "stop immediately." The signal might be visual—a raised hand that means "stop and raise your hand" so that the signal spreads. Or it might be auditory—a whistle or the shouted command "Freeze!" But remember, when we use a whistle for a freeze command, we reserve it for this purpose. Confusion will ensue if the whistle can also mean "go" or "change direction" in a game.

We also need quick ways to gather children for various purposes, perhaps for a reminder or to receive new directions. "Allee! Allee!" is often used as a gathering call. Sometimes, the resulting group is just fine for a quick interaction, letting children know it's time to go in or announcing that teams should switch sides. Other times, when we'll be giving more extensive directions or a demonstration, it's best to have children in a true circle so each child is able to see well and be seen. The command "Circle up!" can invoke this.

Children will not automatically know—and may not remember after they've been shown once—how to freeze, gather, and circle up. So it's essential to model and practice all signals and acceptable responses deliberately and frequently to help keep play safe.

Tagging rules

Since so many games are variations of tag, it's important to teach and regularly remind children about two tagging rules: safe tagging and tagger's choice. Safe tagging can be defined as a gentle, open-handed touch on the shoulder, arm, or back. The jingle "It's a tap or a touch, not a slap or a push" can help children remember. Tagger's choice is a rule that says if the tagger says s/he tagged you, you are tagged. No arguing. Of course, tagger's choice will work only if teachers observe play to make sure the rule isn't abused.

Pairing up and forming small groups

Many games call for children to find a partner or get into groups of three or four. Having students count off, then gather according to their numbers, is one way to ensure that children don't always get together only with their best friends. But there are other interesting ways. Students can line up by height, in birthdate order, or alphabetically by first name, then pair off with the next person in line. Or students can stand in two lines. The two lines walk to meet each other, and the children who end up face-to-face are partners.

Introducing new games

Games—their rules and boundaries and strategies—need to be learned. It's helpful to present new games inside, where children are more attentive. Drawings, diagrams, and instructions help children envision themselves in the game. "Here is where we will play. These are the boundaries. Orlaith's team will be by the building. Their base is here. Shane's team will be by the structure. Their base is here. I will be standing right here. And these are the balls we will use."

Games go more smoothly when teachers talk with the children beforehand about safety issues specific to the particular game being introduced. For example: "There will be lots of people moving fast across the circle. What are some things we can do to keep from crashing into each other?" or "In this game, we'll be trying to get people out by throwing a ball at them. How will we do that so that it'll be fun and safe for everyone?"

The teacher's presence in the game

The teacher's place and presence in a game is critical. This doesn't mean we have to play (though being a player can be an important teacher role) but it does mean we are on active watch. As the children practice the skills of a new game, we observe, remind, and coach. "Remember, Kate, the rule is that the tagger stands five steps away from the safety zone." Or we shout, "Freeze!" And when everyone has frozen, we say, "Everyone needs to throw the ball softly and waist down. Robert, show us. OK, melt and PLAY!"

We know our students—which child might need a quick, quiet reminder and which child might need an encouraging word. "Nice safe tagging, Dominick." "Way to run, Bronagh!" Games are part of active teaching for us. Our students know where our attention is—and where it is not.

Reflecting about games

Talking about games maximizes the learning they offer. So part of playing games is having children practice articulating what made a game work, how they kept it a positive experience for all involved. "What made this game fun?" "Did anybody notice how fast Maurice ran and how loud he yelled when he got caught?" "I saw Caoimhe stop to help Adam get up. And Adam, you smiled." "Did we remember to tag safely? Who had a safe tag?" "Do you think we should play this game tomorrow? How come?"

Through the questions we pose and the comments we offer, we invite and model observation, analysis, and connection. We name positive behaviors we saw, helping children to recognize and name them also. If we noticed that a game wasn't fun, we talk about why and what might make it more fun next time. This reflection helps children see that their actions affect the quality of their play.

Keep playing

Games are a powerful place to teach skills, release and regain energy, and model and build community. So it's important to keep using games, keep talking, keep being playful—and to let ourselves and our students have fun. Our classrooms will be better and our children stronger for having played.

How To Use This Book

The games in this book were chosen because they've been used successfully in a wide variety of K–4 settings. They're easy for teachers to teach and for children to learn. They maximize fun and challenge while minimizing the risk of emotional and physical harm. Some are adaptations of traditional favorites; others are original creations. None require unusual equipment or uncommon skills on the part of the teacher or students. Each game description includes "helpful hints" for making the game run smoothly.

This book is not meant to give you formulas. It's meant to give ideas that you can adapt to fit your needs. If a dish were too spicy for the guests, a chef would adjust the recipe by reducing the spice content. Similarly, if a game seems too energetic for the children you teach, you can change some details to make it less frantic. If your students like challenges, introduce a timed element to see if they can do certain steps faster and faster. If your class needs to play at a slow pace to remain in control, restrict all movement to a walking pace. Write notes and observations in the margins of this book, so that it becomes an ever-growing resource filled with your insights and ideas, your adaptations and creations, as you become a master chef of games.

COOPERATION HOOPS

How to play

1. Children move about the playing area, stepping anywhere except inside a hoop.

2. On a signal from the teacher, everyone finds a hoop and steps inside as quickly as possible, helping each other as needed. To be considered "in" a hoop, a child must have at least one foot in. The other foot may not touch the ground outside the hoop.

3. After everyone is safely in, everyone steps out again, and one hoop is taken away.

Description of game:

In this highly energetic, loud game, the class works together to squeeze as many classmates as possible into a few hula hoops.

Most suitable for:

Kindergartners through 4th graders

Requirements:

- 20 minutes the first time the class plays the game (as little as 5 minutes after they've learned it)

- An indoor or outdoor space big enough for a number of hula hoops to be scattered about without overlapping

- Approximately 1 hula hoop for every 2 children

Pre-game setup:

Scatter the hula hoops on the ground so that they don't overlap and are roughly equidistant from each other. Because children will be moving energetically around the hoops, make sure all hoops are at least 4 feet away from any furniture or other objects.

4. Steps one and two are repeated again and again, with one less hoop each time. Children will have to be inventive and work together to get all players into an ever-decreasing number of hoops.

5. The game continues until children cannot possibly squeeze any more people into the remaining hoops.

Helpful hints

1. Use analogies to connect the game with academics. For example:

   - If the class is studying planets, you can say, "The hoops are planets, and each student is a spaceship flying around the planets. When you hear a warning call of 'Landing!' you must get all the ships to the planets for safety."

   - If you're studying frogs, you can say, "The hoops are lily pads, and each student is a frog swimming around the pads. When the frog lifeguard calls, 'Everyone out of the water!' you need to get all the frogs safely onto the lily pads."

2. For added fun, have children use different movements—walking, hopping, skipping, or moving in slow motion—when weaving around the hoops. Build on your analogy. Students can move like a frog, snake, fish, bear, duck, eagle, or chicken. Use your analogy when taking away the hoops, too. "A huge space monster is gobbling up whole planets," or "A fish is sinking the lily pads." Children will easily get enthusiastic about a wild and crazy idea.

3. Students who are accustomed to competing might have a hard time thinking about how to help each other get inside a hoop, so ask the children to demonstrate how they'll help each other or demonstrate this yourself with another student.

4. Throughout the game, remind the group about helping each other and comment on examples of cooperation that you see.

5. When you've taken away approximately half the hoops, tell students you don't think they can possibly squeeze everyone into fewer hoops, then watch them rise to the challenge. I once saw a group of sixteen kindergartners crammed into one hoop, linking arms, hugging each other, with the outermost layer of children teetering on one foot, and everyone standing on tip-toe to make room.

FOX AND GEESE

How to play

1. The teacher and students create the playing area by tramping out the shape of a large wagon wheel in the snow *(see diagram on next page)*. The teacher can walk out the pattern and the children follow behind in a line, stamping down the snow.

- Make the diameter of the wheel by taking one medium-length adult step (about two feet) for each student participating. Then, make an evenly shaped circle around this diameter line, making sure that the line touches the circle at top and bottom. This line now forms two spokes of the circle.

- Make remaining spokes—about one spoke for every three children in the group. The hub will be the area flattened by making the intersecting spokes.

- Add one or more safety zones outside the wheel to provide a resting spot for out-of-breath children.

Description of game:

This is a highly energetic, boisterous version of tag played in freshly fallen snow. Children run and stumble in clumsy snow gear and get covered in snow.

Most suitable for:

Kindergartners through 4th graders

Requirements:

- 30 minutes (including 10 minutes for marking off the playing area)

- An outdoor space big enough for children to run energetically

- Soft, freshly fallen snow

Pre-game setup:

Marking off the playing area will be part of the game.

2. Children must stay at all times on the wagon-wheel-shaped paths. One to six children volunteer to be the taggers (foxes). They try to tag as many of the other children (the geese) as possible. If a goose who is trying to evade a fox steps off the path, s/he is considered tagged. If a fox steps off the path while trying to tag a goose, the fox must freeze for three seconds and the goose remains untagged.

3. The class chooses one of four options ahead of time for what happens when geese are tagged:

   - **Option 1:** Tagged geese go to the hub of the wheel and stay there until the game ends. Because geese who are tagged early in the game might get restless, the game can end before all geese are caught.

   - **Option 2:** Tagged geese go to the hub of the wheel where they can be freed by other geese who make it to the hub without being tagged. Each rescuer goose can free only one captive. The two must walk hand in hand back to the circumference of the wheel before resuming the game. On this freedom walk, no fox can tag them. (This option works best if there is more than one fox.)

   - **Option 3:** Tagged geese stop where they were tagged and stand with arms raised and legs open wide. Another goose can free a tagged goose by crawling between his/her legs. (Children decked out in snow gear have a lot of fun trying to accomplish this.)

   - **Option 4:** One fox can be a jail guard at the hub, watching over the captured geese. A free goose that gets past the guard and touches one of the captured geese frees all the captives.

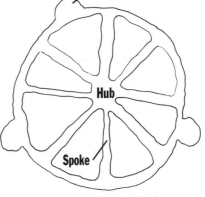

Helpful hints

1. Review safe tagging and tagger's choice. Tagger's choice is particularly important in this game because children will be wearing snow gear, which may make it hard for them to know they've been tagged. Remind children that anyone who steps off the paths will be considered tagged.

2. Introduce this game in the classroom before going out into the snow. If it's your class's first time playing this game, draw a large picture of the wagon wheel so children can picture the playing area.

Diameter equal to approximately one medium-length adult step for each student participating.

CATERPILLAR

Description of game:

Children pretend to be a caterpillar by linking their bodies into a chain and moving forward as a unit in a smooth, coordinated way.

Most suitable for:

Kindergartners through 3rd graders

Requirements:

- 15–30 minutes
- An indoor or outdoor space big enough for several human chains (about eight students each) to move around

Pre-game setup:

If you have gymnastics mats and some benches 8–10 inches tall, set them up as shown on the next page. This will add extra challenge to the game.

How to play

Caterpillar is a great game for building a sense of community. Children learn to move smoothly as a unit by watching and listening to each other and by physically following each other's movements.

1. Children count off to form groups of about eight. From either a standing or a kneeling position, each member of the group holds on to the person in front to form a "caterpillar." If kneeling, they hold the ankles of the person in front. If standing, they simply hold the elbows or waist of the person in front.

2. The caterpillars move around the playing area. The goal is to move in a smooth, coordinated way. If there are mats and benches set up, the caterpillars can climb or crawl up and over the benches.

3. Every few minutes, the first child in each caterpillar goes to the back of the chain, allowing each student a chance to lead.

Helpful hints

1. To introduce the game in a fun way, tell the class you're thinking of a creature and you need their help to remember what it's called. Give clues. "This creature has lots of legs." "This creature grows up to be a beautiful butterfly." "This creature begins with the letter *C*."

2. Ask the class to think about how a caterpillar's many legs work together smoothly. To demonstrate, ask one child from each group to come forward. These children form a chain and try to move as a unit. If their movement is awkward, ask the class to coach them on how to move more smoothly.

3. When this "short caterpillar" is able to move relatively smoothly, have the children make a "long caterpillar" in their own groups and repeat what the short caterpillar did. Chances are the movements will be very awkward at first if children are in a kneeling position. Caterpillars will break apart and children will tip over. Encourage children to keep trying, offering suggestions if needed. For example, you might suggest that children talk to each other or that the leader of each caterpillar wait until everyone is ready before starting to move forward.

4. After a short while, stop the action. Ask children to share what's hard about moving as a unit and what seems to help. For example, you might ask, "Is it easier if you watch the person in front of you closely? Which is easier—when the first person in the caterpillar moves quickly or moves slowly?"

5. Have children go back to their caterpillar positions to try again. Give lots of encouragement and soon the caterpillars will be cruising around the room.

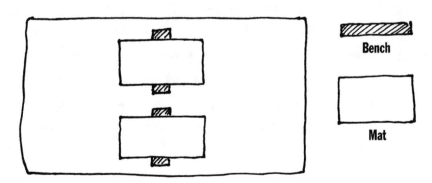

The benches are set under the mats.

HUMAN ALPHABET

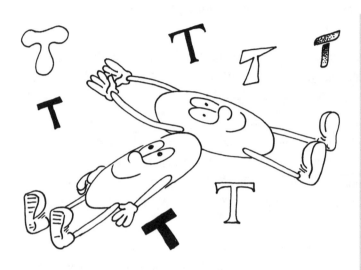

Description of game:

Working together, children use their bodies to form letters and simple words on the floor. There will be lots of talking and demonstrating as children plan how to form the letters and words.

Most suitable for:

1st through 4th graders

Requirements:

- 25 minutes
- An indoor space big enough for children to lie down and spread out

Pre-game setup:

None

How to play

1. Children pair up and lie down on the floor. The teacher calls out an easy-to-form letter such as *V*. Working with their partner, children use their bodies to form that letter on the floor. The teacher then calls out another easy-to-form letter, such as *T, L,* or *O*.

2. After a few letters, the pairs of children join to form groups of four. This time the teacher calls out more complicated letters—such as *W, M, P, H*—and each foursome forms these letters.

3. Finally, children get into groups of about ten to spell out simple words that the teacher chooses. Examples are WALK, TALK, TALL, TAIL, TOIL, SOIL. (Note that only one letter changes at a time in this progression, though eventually every letter changes.)

Helpful hints

1. Help students visualize large letters by having them write their names in the air. Demonstrate with your own name, using big sweeping arm movements and a "magic air pencil."

2. Next, have children use their feet to write their name on the floor. They can trace out the shape of the letters by shuffling their feet, walking, or running.

3. After the pairs of students have formed a few easy letters using their whole bodies, stop and acknowledge what you see. Ask children what helped them. Listen for—and gently direct students' attention toward—responses that show constructive conversation and teamwork. "Oh, so you had a plan as to who would be the top of the T and who would be the stem?" or "Dane, you and Gerard decided that your feet would be at the bottom of the V and your heads would be at the top?" Continue to talk about helpful strategies throughout the game.

4. In a variation of the game, students form numbers instead of letters. Students work in pairs to form single-digit numbers, then in larger groups to form double-digit numbers. Later, you can even have children reply to simple math questions by forming the answers with their bodies.

Be sure to test out a game before introducing it to children. This gives you a sense of the game's mood and lets you better anticipate the children's behavior. Staff meetings provide a great opportunity to try out games. You'll have fun—and your peers can help with management strategies.

ROCK, PAPER, SCISSORS

How to play

We've all played Rock, Paper, Scissors sometime in our life. Some of us still use it with our friends when we can't agree on something and don't have a coin to flip. It's an old classic that's not only fun in its own right, but an element of several other games in this book.

1. Children pair off and sit or stand facing each other. Using an agreed upon count-in *("1-2-3-Go!" or "Rock-Paper-Scissors-Go!"),* the two children each show a hand symbol on the word *"Go!"* Children may choose the symbol for rock, the symbol for paper, or the symbol for scissors.

2. Each child has an equal chance of winning because each symbol can beat and be beaten by another symbol. Rock crushes scissors; scissors cut paper; paper covers rock. If both children show the same symbol, they go again.

3. Children change partners often to keep the game fresh.

Description of game:

Hand signals and chance determine who wins and who loses in this classic game.

Most suitable for:

Kindergartners through 4th graders

Requirements:

- 10 minutes if children are playing this for the first time (much shorter if they already know the game)

- An indoor or outdoor space big enough to allow children to sit or stand in pairs

Pre-game setup:

None

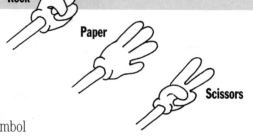

Helpful hints

1. If children are unfamiliar with this game, be sure to demonstrate each symbol *(see diagram on previous page)*. To practice, flash a symbol with your hand and ask them to show you the symbol that beats it. Continue with this until children have the rules down pat. This practice session also shows that this is a game of pure chance.

2. Emphasize gentle, careful play. Demonstrate how rock *gently* taps scissors, how scissors *gently* makes the motion of cutting paper, and how paper *gently* wraps around rock. Or, you may simply make a rule that a child can't touch another child's hands.

3. If children are brand new to this game, start with the *"1-2-3-Go!"* count-in. I've found that if beginners count in with *"Rock-Paper-Scissors-Go!"* they often forget which symbol they intended to show.

4. For added style, children can tap one fist against the other palm or clap their hands to the beat during the count-in.

5. For added challenge, children could try using another language for the count-in. For example, *"Uno-Dos-Tres-Anda!"*

Joining in a game as a player—being a teammate—is perhaps my favorite thing to do when it comes to games. I love the high fives (or medium fives if working with kindergartners), the smiles, and the sense of connection that develops between teacher and children.

TEAM ROCK, PAPER, SCISSORS

How to play

Tagging as a team, switching sides, and relying on chance to determine taggers all help children focus on fun rather than competition.

1. Students count off to form two teams, one of which will be the taggers. To decide which team will tag, children play a team version of Rock, Paper, Scissors with everyone on a team flashing the same symbol against the other team.

2. Each team needs to choose two symbols to use for Rock, Paper, Scissors in case the first one results in a tie. The teams huddle at opposite ends of the playing area to decide on their two symbols.

Description of game:

In this version of tag, everyone on one team tries to tag players on the other team.

Most suitable for:

Kindergartners through 4th graders

Requirements:

- 20 minutes
- An open area, ideally outdoors, big enough to allow children to move energetically
- Six cones, flags, or other markers
- Enough rope to indicate a center line
- Children need to know how to play Rock, Paper, Scissors (see page 14)

Pre-game setup:

Mark off the playing area. *(See diagram on the next page.)*

Rock

Paper

Scissors

3. The two teams then line up facing each other at the center line. Using an agreed-upon count-in *("1-2-3-Go!"* or *"Rock-Paper-Scissors-Go!")*, all players flash their team's symbol at the same time. The winning team become the taggers. The tagging begins as soon as children see which team won.

4. Children who are tagged must join the tagging team. Those who reach the safety zone cannot be tagged.

5. When everyone has either been tagged or has reached the safety zone, another round of the game begins with Rock, Paper, Scissors. Team composition will have changed since some players were tagged in the first game and changed sides.

Helpful hints

1. Review how to play Rock, Paper, Scissors. The review is an opportunity for you to emphasize playing in a caring and safe way. See "Helpful hints" (p. 15) in the description of Rock, Paper, Scissors.

2. In twenty minutes of play, there will be many chances to choose team symbols to use for Rock, Paper, Scissors. This lets children practice making group decisions in a fair and fun way. But sometimes the loudest, most dominant students will force their will onto the group. To head this off, brainstorm with the children fair and fun ways to decide on their team's symbol. You may be surprised by the imaginative solutions they come up with. Be ready to offer some ideas yourself, if needed. Here are two possibilities:

- Everyone on the team flashes a symbol using a count-in; the symbol that the majority of players show is the symbol the team uses.

- Two people on the team play Rock, Paper, Scissors against each other. The winning symbol is the one the team uses.

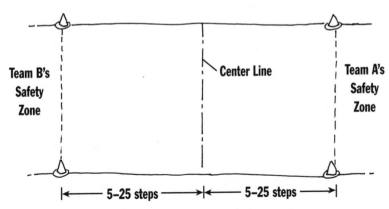

The playing area should be wide enough that one team can stand with arms outstretched fingertip to fingertip.

ODDS AND EVENS

How to play

When children play this game over and over—as many as ten games in a minute—the transience of victory and defeat helps them see that the fun of playing a game is more important than who wins and who loses.

Description of game:

This is a simple, quick game, similar to Rock, Paper, Scissors, in which the winner is determined by pure chance.

Most suitable for:

1st through 4th graders

Requirements:

- 5–15 minutes
- An indoor or outdoor space big enough to allow children to sit or stand in pairs
- Children need to know the concept of odd and even numbers

Pre-game setup:

None

1. Children pair off and say in unison, *"0-1-2-Go!"* On *"Go!"* they each show zero, one, or two fingers.

2. Prior to the count-in, one child in each pair guesses that the total number of fingers shown by the two children will be an odd number. The other child guesses that it will be an even number. Whoever guessed correctly is the winner. If both children show zero, they play again.

3. Each pair of children play several games, taking turns on who guesses first. After about a minute, children change partners to keep the game fresh.

Helpful hints

1. For added fun and style, children can tap out the rhythm of *"0-1-2-Go!"* as they chant the phrase.

2. Be aware that older children may use their middle finger to show one finger. If you think this will be a problem with your group, talk with the children about which gestures are OK and which are not.

3. Students may figure out that they can win by slightly delaying their gesture. For example, if Therese calls even, she could wait until Niall begins to show two fingers before gesturing with zero or two fingers. To prevent this, talk with students about the importance of making their gesture exactly at "Go."

4. This activity is not only fun in itself, but it can also be used to determine who's "it" in a game, who makes the first move, and so forth. It also reinforces the math concept of odd and even numbers.

Let yourself have fun when playing games with children. When children sense that you're enjoying the game, they'll enjoy it, too.

ROB THE ROOSTER

How to play

1. Children stand in a tight circle, shoulder to shoulder, with one child in the middle of the circle.

2. The children in the circle pass an object, named "Rob the Rooster," around the circle behind their backs so that it's hard for the child in the middle to see who has Rob. As students pass Rob around, they chant, "Rob the Rooster, keep it going, keep it going. Rob the Rooster, keep it going, keep it going…." To make it more difficult to guess who has Rob, students can move their arms rhythmically behind their backs throughout the game. The arms begin close to the body so that both hands are touching each other. Then the arms open out so that each child's right arm is behind the person to the right and the left arm is behind the person to the left.

3. When the child in the middle has an idea where Rob is, s/he raises a hand to stop the action and make a guess. After each incorrect guess, Rob travels again and the children continue to chant. The guesser can have up to three guesses. If the child locates Rob (or is unable to locate Rob after three guesses), s/he takes a place in the circle and a new child, chosen by the teacher, comes into the middle.

Helpful hints

1. In introducing the game, tell children that there is a rooster named Rob who likes to stay hidden. He also likes to be sung to and his favorite song is aptly named after him.

2. Have children practice the "Rob the Rooster" chant and arm movements before beginning the game. Remind the children that Rob must always travel behind their backs and that they must try and pass him on as quickly as possible.

3. You should always decide which child is the guesser. Tying that decision to being in possession of Rob changes the nature of the activity.

4. Once you have selected the guesser, have that child close her/his eyes and turn around a few times while you give Rob to someone. When the group starts singing, the guesser can open her/his eyes and try to find Rob.

5. Based on your group, decide if there should be a time limit for making a guess.

6. Remind the group that when the guesser raises a hand, the singing and passing of Rob must stop and all children must bring their hands behind their own backs.

7. Keep framing the win-loss as Rob versus the group. "And Rob the sneaky rooster wins again!" "Aha! We caught Rob! He'll have to work harder next time to stay hidden."

CiRCLE SWAP

How to play

1. Children stand in a circle and point to the person they believe is directly opposite them in the circle.

2. On a signal, each child must swap places with her/his opposite by going through the middle of the circle without bumping anyone.

3. If two children identify the same person as their opposite, they simply try to end up next to each other in that person's spot.

4. If a child is bumped, s/he says "BEEP." The challenge is to make the grand swap without a sound.

Helpful hints

1. Before beginning, emphasize the goal of completing the swap without a single "BEEP." Ask students to suggest strategies that might be helpful in avoiding crashes. Acknowledge strategies that involve watching, waiting, and stopping when needed.

2. Monitor this game carefully, especially during the first few rounds. If there are students who intentionally bump into others, be sure to stop the game immediately and address the problem.

3. Once children begin to get the hang of it, they can try to do the swap within a time limit, say ten seconds. After a few more rounds, try having them pick two spots on the opposite side of the circle and travel to first one, then the other, within a time limit.

Description of game:

In this fast-moving game, children try to swap places in a circle without bumping into each other.

Most suitable for:

Kindergartners through 4th graders

Requirements:

- 10 minutes
- Any indoor or outdoor space big enough for children to stand in a circle

Pre-game setup:

None

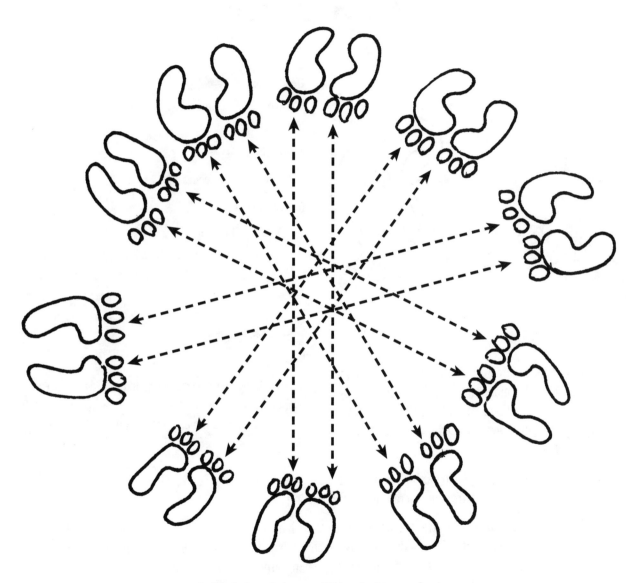

In this fast-moving game, children try to swap places
in a circle without bumping into each other.

GAA GAA

How to play

This game was created by students of Greenfield Center School, the independent K–8 school established by Northeast Foundation for Children. Unlike traditional dodgeball, everyone tries to get everyone out in this game.

Description of game:

A version of dodgeball, this game is fast-paced, highly energetic, and loud.

Most suitable for:

2nd through 4th graders

Requirements:

- 5–20 minutes
- An indoor or outdoor area free of obstacles and big enough for children to move around energetically
- A partially deflated playground ball or other soft ball

Pre-game setup:

Clearly define the boundaries of the playing area. For example, lay down gym mats to form the playing area or use box benches to enclose the area.

1. All players get into the playing area. The teacher starts the game with a serve, which consists of rolling the ball into the playing area from any spot outside the playing area.

2. Players then throw, roll, or hit the ball around with their hands or arms, trying to get others out. The hands and arms are the only parts of the body that may touch the ball. If the ball touches any other part of a player's body, he or she is out and must stand outside the playing area. The only exception occurs with a serve—no player can be out from a serve.

3. If someone catches a fly ball before it touches the floor, the person who threw or hit the ball is out.

4. If the ball goes out of the playing area, the teacher (or a child who's out and standing outside the perimeter) simply rolls it back in.

Helpful hints

1. Because this is a fast game with children jumping and scuttling about, you will have to remain vigilant as a referee and protector. Here are additional rules that I use to keep the game from getting too rambunctious and therefore dangerous:

   - Players must remain on their feet at all times. No crawling, donkey kicks, etc.

   - Only hands and feet may touch the floor. If any other body part touches the floor, the player is out.

   - Only throw the ball at people from the shoulders down.

   - If the ball hits—or almost hits—a player's head, the person who threw the ball is out. I don't allow the excuse "I didn't mean it" because I want children to be aware of the possible results of their actions, even in the adrenaline-charged action of a game.

2. Adjust rules for your group as needed. But remember, even if the children helped change the rules, you are still the game's referee and rule-enforcer.

3. When playing indoors, I always insist that children take off their shoes to avoid squished fingers and toes.

4. I never let the game get to a point where there's only one winner. When there are a few players left, I give a ten-second warning. When the ten seconds are up, I start a new game. This also helps keep the games short so that the children who are out don't become bored and fidgety.

FiND YOUR PARTNER

HOT? COLD?

How to play

This game challenges children to listen, concentrate, and help each other so trust can develop.

1. The group circles up, then counts off to form groups of three.

Description of game:

Wearing blindfolds, children find their partner by following the sound of his/her voice.

Most suitable for:

Kindergartners through 4th graders

Requirements:

- 20 minutes
- An indoor or outdoor space, free of obstacles (indoor is best for kindergartners through 2nd graders)
- Enough blindfolds for 2 out of every 3 children
- Index cards (for kindergartners through 2nd graders)

Pre-game setup:

Make sure the playing area is free of obstacles, bumps, or holes.

2. Each group chooses or is assigned a partner name.
   Partner names consist of two words that have a relationship to each other, such as "Hot and Cold." Other examples of partner names are "Big and Small," "Pen and Pencil," or "School and Bus."

3. In each group, two of the children put on blindfolds. The third acts as a safety. The safety guides the two blindfolded children to two different locations in the playing area, relatively far apart from each other.

4. On the teacher's signal, the blindfolded children try to find their partners by calling out the predetermined name. They are not allowed to say anything other than the name. For example, in a pair named "Hot and Cold," one child calls out "Hot" and his/her partner answers "Cold."

5. Only one of the partners moves; the other blindfolded partner stays in one spot. The safety stays near the moving partner.

6. The safety's job is to make sure that the moving partner doesn't go out of bounds or get into danger.

7. When all partners have found each other, children get back into their groups of three, and a new child in the threesome becomes the safety. The game repeats until all children have had a chance to be a safety.

Helpful hints

1. Before playing, talk about how to keep the game safe and fun for everyone. For example, blindfolded children will need to listen very carefully. Safeties will need to look for objects and/or people that the blindfolded children could bump into and guide the children gently to safety. When guiding someone, safeties should use a firm but gentle hand on the shoulder and talk to the person. You might want to model appropriate guiding.

2. Some children, especially younger ones, might find it frightening to be blindfolded. Let these children act as the safeties first. Seeing the game played safely may encourage them to try on the blindfolds themselves—but you should never require them to do so.

3. Part of the fun of the game is using quirky partner names. If you're teaching an older class, let the children pick their own names, then check for the appropriateness of their choices. With younger children, you can write partner names on index cards, then have each group draw a card.

4. In an older class, you may want to let groups adopt a new name for each round of play (each time there's a new safety).

MIRROR GAME

How to play

Description of game:

In pairs, children act as mirror reflections of each other.

Most suitable for:

Kindergartners through 4th graders

Requirements:

- 10–30 minutes
- Any indoor or outdoor space that's large enough for pairs of children to work without distracting other pairs

Pre-game setup:

None

Empathy is perhaps the hardest skill to "teach" children. While this game doesn't try to teach empathy, it allows children to practice watching another's actions and expressions closely, which is part of being empathetic.

1. Children pair up. Each pair goes to a spot in the room where they won't distract others.

2. The children in each pair stand facing one another. One child makes a series of motions—squatting down, standing up, turning around, waving, etc.—and the other child copies the motions as if s/he were a mirror reflection.

3. After both children have led a few times, they come up with a short skit that includes a sequence of steps, such as brushing teeth, washing face, combing hair, making toast, eating toast, cleaning up after eating. Pairs can volunteer to perform their skit for the class and children can guess what they're doing.

Helpful hints

1. To introduce this game, have children circle up and tell them to copy everything you say or do until you say "Stop!" Do a variety of things—stand up, sit down, turn around, run in place, scratch your ear, or do the twist. When all the children seem to understand, call "Stop!" and get them into pairs.

2. Next, model mirroring with a student, with you taking the lead. Make your movements slow and large. Ask the group what they noticed and emphasize that slow and large movements will make it easier for partners to mirror.

3. Also before beginning, establish the following rules:

   - Children must do the activity silently—no words or other sounds.

   - Children are to remain on their own side of the "mirror."

   - Children should be able to do the movement without falling.

4. Throughout the game, walk around and comment when children are well synchronized or show high levels of creativity or concentration. At the same time, redirect inappropriate behavior.

5. As an alternative game, ask children to mirror emotions rather than actions. One child in each pair expresses an emotion with her/his face and body. In addition to copying the facial expressions and body language, the other child tries to recognize and name the emotion. Then the children switch roles. The guessing and role-switches should happen quickly.

TiME FOR BED

How to play

Description of game:

This is a "whodunit" in which students need to guess who's giving the secret handshake that puts people to sleep.

Most suitable for:

2nd through 4th graders

Requirements:

- 10–20 minutes
- An indoor space big enough for children to move around freely and to lie down

Pre-game setup:

None

This game is based on the old favorite, Murder in the Dark (or Assassin), but avoids references to violence and death.

1. While the children lie facedown on the floor with their eyes covered, the teacher walks around the group and touches one child's head. That child will be the Sleep Wizard.

2. Students stand. All students mill about shaking hands. The child chosen to be the Sleep Wizard, however, uses a special handshake, such as one with two firm squeezes. This special handshake must be subtle, only able to be detected by those who receive it and not by observers.

3. Those who receive the special handshake must lie down and pretend to go to sleep.

4. Other children try to guess who the Sleep Wizard is before receiving the special handshake. If a child makes a guess and is wrong, s/he joins the sleeping children on the floor.

Helpful hints

1. Demonstrate and have students practice the actions involved in the game before they start playing:

   - *The standard handshake:* While this a simple enough action, modeling and practicing it will help students differentiate it from the Sleep Wizard's special handshake.

   - *The Sleep Wizard's handshake:* Emphasize the importance of the Sleep Wizard giving two firm, distinct squeezes so children will know for sure when they've been given the signal. Have students partner up and practice giving each other the Sleep Wizard's handshake.

   - *Going to sleep:* Yawn and stretch, then slowly and safely lie down on the floor. Ask students what they noticed about how you stayed safe—you lay down quietly and calmly, you made sure the floor was clear, and you lowered your body in a controlled way.

2. During the game, there will be a lot of people lying on the floor. Ask, "What do we need to do so that every-one will be safe? What do people who are 'asleep' need to do? What do those walking around need to do?"

   - Students lying down need to keep their hands and feet to themselves, stay quiet, and not toss and turn.

   - Students walking around need to walk slowly, walk around rather than over those lying down, and steer wide of the "sleepers" to avoid stepping on fingers, hair, etc.

3. To keep children from guessing who was picked, I talk as I walk through the group. I also bend down several times both before and after I've chosen the Sleep Wizard.

"My Bonny Lies over the ocean"

My Bonny lies over the ocean...

My Bonny ... the sea...

How to play

This is a great activity to do when the class needs a quick energizer.

1. Children get in a circle and sing the song "My Bonny Lies Over the Ocean."

2. Each time the *B* sound occurs in the song, everyone makes an agreed-upon body motion—for example, standing up at the first *B* sound, sitting down at the next *B* sound, standing up again at the next, and so forth. Other possible motions include arms up, then arms down, and jumping to face backward, then jumping to face forward.

3. As the children get the hang of the game, they sing the song faster and faster. Or they can choose different body movements to try.

Helpful hints

1. Here are the words to the song, in case the class needs to learn it:

   My Bonny lies over the ocean.
   My Bonny lies over the sea.
   My Bonny lies over the ocean,
   So bring back my Bonny to me.
   Bring back, bring back,
   Oh bring back my Bonny to me, to me.
   Bring back, bring back,
   Oh bring back my Bonny to me.

2. When introducing the game to kindergartners and first graders, who are often excited about the fact that they know the alphabet, I ask them to think about all the words they know that begin with the letter *B*. The list they come up with is quite impressive.

3. For second through fourth graders, the alphabet is old news. In introducing the game to this age group, you may want to focus on the movements that accompany the song and offer a challenge such as, "Let's see how quickly you can sing the song and still make the body movements at the correct times?"

4. Regardless of age group, begin the song slowly so children can experience success. With younger children, you may want to use hand signals to help them remember when to make the body movements. Speed up the song only when the group is getting the hang of it.

5. It's okay if everyone doesn't end up in the same position, as long as children are trying to make the body movements at the right times. After all, part of the fun is seeing half the group in one position and half in the other at the end of the song.

Did you know that this song is about a historic figure?
"Bonny" is Charles Edward Stuart. Nicknamed Bonny Prince Charlie,
he led the Scots in an unsuccessful rebellion against the British throne
in 1745–1746. Afterward, he fled to Europe to avoid capture.

EVOLUTION

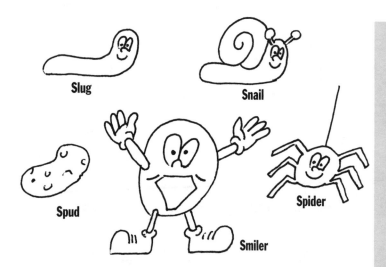

Slug

Snail

Spud

Spider

Smiler

How to play

1. The class names six animals that can be arranged in some kind of progression, such as small to large or slow to fast. For example:

   ■ *Small to large:* flea—mouse—cat—cow—elephant—whale

   ■ *Slow to fast:* snail—tortoise—snake—pig—dog—horse

2. Children move around the room pretending to be the first animal in their list, for example, a flea if the class chose the small-to-large list above. Children may use actions and animal sounds, but they may not speak.

3. Next, each child goes up to another student and plays Rock, Paper, Scissors or Odds and Evens. The winner "evolves" into the next animal in the list—a mouse in this example—and moves around the room pretending to be a mouse, while the child who lost continues his/her journey as a flea.

Description of game:

Children use body movements and sounds to imitate animals. Challenging each other with repeated games of Rock, Paper, Scissors or Odds and Evens, they "evolve" from one animal to another.

Most suitable for:

2nd through 4th graders

Requirements:

■ 5–10 minutes

■ An indoor space big enough for children to move around freely

■ A large easel chart pad or blackboard

■ Children must know how to play Rock, Paper, Scissors (see page 14) or Odds and Evens (see page 18)

Pre-game setup:

None

4. Now the mouse finds another mouse with whom to play Rock, Paper, Scissors or Odds and Evens, and the winner evolves into a cat. Meanwhile, the flea must find another flea and win one of the games before evolving into a mouse.

5. The game continues, with like animals finding each other to see who gets to evolve into the next animal. Two different animals may not play against each other.

Helpful hints

1. Before playing, have the group come up with actions and sounds for each animal so children can recognize each other. Start the game only after children have practiced these actions and sounds and are clear on the progression of animals. Write the progression of animals on an easel pad or blackboard.

2. Be aware that in every game some children will be left with no way to evolve into the next animal on the list. For example, if there are six animals on the list, five students won't be able to find another like animal and, therefore, won't be able to move to the next stage. In these cases, a tap on the head from the teacher can allow a child to evolve to the next stage. Also, play the game several times to give everyone more chances to achieve complete evolution.

If I know it will take more than three minutes to introduce a game and model appropriate behaviors, I'll save it until after the class has played other games that use some of the same skills. When you say, "Let's play a game," children get excited. If the introduction takes too long, their energy will bubble over, often not in a constructive way.

SEVEN UP

How to play

1. All but seven children sit at tables or desks with their heads down, eyes covered, and one thumb up.

2. The seven children walk around, each choosing one of the seated children, and gently push that child's thumb down. When all seven are done, they line up in front of the group and say together, "Seven Up!"

3. Each child whose thumb was pushed down guesses who the "thumb pusher" was. The thumb pusher doesn't say whether or not the guess was correct until all children have guessed. At that point, the teacher asks who pushed each

Description of game:

This quick guess-who-tapped-you game is a good way to fill that 5-minute gap between activities.

Most suitable for:

1st through 4th graders

Requirements:

- 5–10 minutes
- An indoor space where some of the class can sit at tables or desks and some can walk around in front of them

Pre-game setup:

None

child's thumb. If a child guessed correctly, the child and the thumb pusher switch places. If the guess is incorrect, the child stays seated. Each child gets only one guess.

4. After everyone has guessed, the seven children standing in front are the thumb pushers for the next round of play. A group of twenty children should be able to play about three rounds in five minutes once they're familiar with the game.

Helpful hints

1. Before playing, teach and model how to push another child's thumb down in a gentle way. Let students practice quickly.

2. Be aware of the children who still have not had their thumbs pushed down after several rounds. To give them more action, you can pick a new set of seven thumb pushers that includes these children. If you know beforehand that certain children are likely to be left out, you can deliberately pick these children to be the thumb pushers in the first round. Also, before starting, emphasize that it's important to choose different people's thumbs to push down so that the game is fun for everyone.

3. Children can continue this game from one day to the next. The seven children left standing at the end of one day would be the seven who start the next day. A simple list posted in the classroom will help everyone remember who the seven starters are.

4. This game can be played with fewer than seven thumb pushers. I wouldn't go above seven, though, because that will make it too hard for children to guess who pushed their thumb.

WINTER BLITZ

How to play

Description of game:

This snow-moving contest serves as an alternative to snowball throwing.

Most suitable for:

Kindergartners through 4th graders

Requirements:

- 10–15 minutes
- A large outdoor area
- Soft, freshly fallen snow
- A length of rope that is long enough to divide the playing field in half

Pre-game setup:

Use the rope to mark a dividing line across the playing area. *(See diagram on next page)*

At the sight of freshly fallen snow, students inevitably end up in snowball fights if left to invent their own games. The problem with snowballs is that we all love throwing them but hate being hit by them. Winter Blitz allows children to play in the snow and blow off energy without resorting to snowball fights.

1. Students count off to form two teams. The two teams stand facing each other on opposite sides of the dividing line.

2. On the teacher's signal, each team moves as much snow as it can across the line to the other side. Students may use any method to move the snow *except* making and throwing snowballs.

3. When the teacher yells "Freeze!" students step away from the line to let the teacher judge which team has less snow on its side. That team is the winner of this round.

4. In each subsequent round, the group decides on one method of snow moving that everyone must use. For example, players may only push the snow with their hands in one round, use only their feet in another round, and only shove the snow between their legs in yet another round.

Helpful hints

1. Before starting the game, talk with students about safety. You might say, "It's a lot of fun to tumble and roll around with each other in snow. It's also important that no one gets hurt. What are some rules we'll need to keep this game fun and safe for everyone?"

2. Each round of play should be fairly short—about two minutes. This will keep the game moving and children's energy level high.

3. Here's one way to decide which snow moving methods to use in the later rounds: After the first "free choice" round, ask students to describe and demonstrate some of the methods they used. Use one of their methods for each subsequent round until all the methods have been used or until you run out of time.

4. In my experience, it can be almost impossible to really determine which team has moved more snow. Team A will move a pile of snow and then Team B will move it right back again. Use this to your advantage to declare alternate winners.

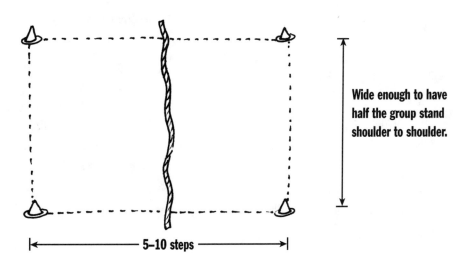

Wide enough to have half the group stand shoulder to shoulder.

|← 5–10 steps →|

PARTNER TAG

1...2...3...Tag!
1...2...3...Tag!
1...2...3...Tag!
1...2...3...Tag!
1...2...3...Tag!
1...2...3...Tag!

How to play

1. Children partner up and decide which child in the pair will be the first tagger.

2. Children may tag only their partners. For example, Regina may tag only Darren, and Darren may tag only Regina.

3. When a partner is tagged, s/he becomes the tagger. The new tagger must give his/her partner a three-second lead.

4. Children may not run in this game. All movement must be no faster than a fast walk.

5. The game continues with partners switching roles back and forth.

The following tag games are listed in the order of difficulty. I recommend that children master the skills in one game before moving on to the next.

PARTNER TAG
ISLAND TAG
TOILET TAG
UNDER THE BRIDGE
COMPOST HEAD
CAPTURE THE FLAG

Description of game:

Partners try to tag each other in this very active tag game.

Most suitable for:

Kindergartners through 4th graders

Requirements:

- 5–20 minutes
- An indoor or outdoor space with clearly marked boundaries that's big enough for children to move about at a fast walking pace. A space the size of half a basketball court would be ideal for a group of 20 children.

Pre-game setup:

None

Helpful hints

1. Review safe tagging and tagger's choice. Remind children that anyone who steps outside of the boundaries of the playing area will be considered tagged.

2. You'll need to be extra vigilant about safety because children will be so focused on their partners that they may bump into each other if they're not careful.

3. Here are some variations on the basic game:

   - Instead of just counting to three, taggers can spin around three times or sit down and stand up three times.

   - Children can play this as a running game once they're familiar with it. For safety, triple the size of the playing area.

   - The game can be played in groups of three, where A always tags B, B always tags C, and C always tags A. Be sure to reverse the order of the tagging periodically so that A→B→C→A becomes C→B→A→C.

   - To add to younger children's enjoyment of the game, you might have all the taggers pretend to be one animal and all the non-taggers pretend to be another animal. During the game, children make the animals' sounds, so that you have elephants chasing ducks, sheep chasing cats, frogs chasing dogs, chickens chasing horses, or any other silly combination.

4. When assigning partners, consider children's running abilities. If a very fast runner is paired with a slow runner, the slow child might feel frustrated at never catching her/his partner. Also, change partners frequently to keep the game fresh.

I personally don't like to have children tag each other on exposed skin. When you're moving fast, even a tap that was meant to be gentle can hurt enough to be unpleasant.

iSLAND TAG

How to play

1. Children pair up and then the partners stand side by side in a large circle. Partners link arms so that each pair forms an "island" in the circle.

2. The teacher chooses one pair of children to start the game and decides which of the two children will be the tagger.

3. The pair of children begin running around the outside of the circle, with the tagger trying to catch his or her partner after giving the partner a three-second lead. If the tagger succeeds, the children reverse roles.

4. At any time, the child being chased can join one of the "islands" in the circle to be "safe." When this happens, the child at the other end of the island breaks away and becomes the one being chased. This child must then join a different island to be safe.

Helpful hints

1. Review safe tagging and tagger's choice before starting the game.

The following tag games are listed in the order of difficulty. I recommend that children master the skills in one game before moving on to the next.

PARTNER TAG
iSLAND TAG
ToiLET TAG
UNDER THE BRiDGE
COMPOST HEAP
CAPTURE THE FLAG

Description of game:

In this tag game, only two people are running at a time. All children will be focused on the game, however, because at any moment they could become part of the fray.

Most suitable for:

1st through 4th graders

Requirements:

- 5–20 minutes
- An indoor or outdoor space big enough for children to form a large standing circle with 2 children running around the outside of the circle

Pre-game setup:

None

2. Some children will want to continue running rather than find safety in the circle. To prevent this, set a ten-second limit on how long children can run before they must attach themselves to an "island."

3. Another potential problem is that some of the children will always choose the same pairs in the circle, keeping the rest of the class from being involved. Generally, you can prevent this by reminding the class beforehand to include everyone in friendly play. However, be ready to remind and redirect individual children as needed during the game.

4. To help children practice self-control, make a rule that runners may not touch children in the circle in any way except to link arms as they attach themselves to an "island."

TOILET TAG

WHOOOOOOSH

How to play

This game is lots of fun to both play and observe. Kids get a big kick out of pretending to be a flushing toilet.

1. One child is the tagger and tries to tag as many people as possible.

2. Any child who is tagged must freeze and raise one arm. The tagged child must stay in this position until freed by another player.

3. To free a tagged child, a player must take that person's raised arm (the toilet handle) and pull it down, at which point the tagged child loudly says, "Whoosh!" (the flush).

The following tag games are listed in the order of difficulty. I recommend that children master the skills in one game before moving on to the next.

PARTNER TAG
ISLAND TAG
TOILET TAG
UNDER THE BRIDGE
COMPOST HEAD
CAPTURE THE FLAG

Description of game:

In this fast-moving, humorous tag game, a child who frees a tagged player is rewarded by the whooshing sound of a flushing toilet.

Most suitable for:

Kindergartners through 4th graders

Requirements:

- 5–25 minutes
- An indoor or outdoor space, with clearly marked boundaries, that's big enough for children to run around safely

Pre-game setup:

None

Helpful hints

1. Review safe tagging and tagger's choice. Remind children that anyone who steps outside the boundaries of the playing area will be considered tagged.

2. If it seems like almost everyone is free even though the tagger is catching a lot of children, add a second, third, or fourth tagger. Be sure to let everyone know about the addition. Nothing feels more unfair to a child than being caught by someone who they didn't know was a tagger.

Whenever you need to speak with a child during a game to give a reminder about rules or redirect behavior, stand so that you face the action while the child has his/her back to it. This helps the child focus on you while allowing you to continue observing the game.

UNDER THE BRIDGE

How to play

This game is very similar to Toilet Tag. However, freeing a tagged player requires a bigger risk in this game because rescuers need to stop moving, get down on all fours, crawl through another's legs, and stand back up before the tagger gets to them. I like to have a discussion with the children about how taking a risk to help a friend can be very rewarding.

1. One child is the tagger and tries to tag as many people as possible.

2. Any child who is tagged must stop moving and stand with legs wide apart to make a "bridge" until s/he is freed by another player.

The following tag games are listed in the order of difficulty. I recommend that children master the skills in one game before moving on to the next.

PARTNER TAG
ISLAND TAG
TOILET TAG
UNDER THE BRIDGE
COMPOST HEAD
CAPTURE THE FLAG

Description of game:

This fast-moving tag game requires children to perform a fairly hard task to free captured players.

Most suitable for:

1st through 4th graders

Requirements:

- 10–25 minutes

- An indoor or outdoor space with clearly marked boundaries, big enough for children to run around

- Cones or ropes to mark the boundaries

Pre-game setup:

None

3. To free a tagged child, a player must crawl under the bridge.

Helpful hints

1. Review safe tagging and tagger's choice. Remind children that anyone who steps outside the boundaries of the playing area will be considered tagged.

2. If it seems like almost everyone is free even though the tagger is catching a lot of children, add a second tagger. I rarely have more than two taggers in this game, as I want to make it possible for tagged children to be freed. If you add a tagger, be sure to let everyone know. Nothing feels more unfair to a child than being caught by someone who they didn't know was a tagger.

In any game of tag, try to change taggers often. This prevents children from getting frustrated by having to keep chasing after others or by being constantly chased. Changing roles often can also keep the game more lively and challenging.

COMPOST HEAP

How to play

This is an advanced-level tag game that requires children to keep constant track of who can tag whom.

1. The group forms two teams. Each team stands in its safety zone (garden).

2. At any time, children may step out of the garden into the tag zone to begin the game. There's no rule or order for how to do this. Each child enters the tag zone when s/he feels ready.

3. Those who are in the tag zone may be tagged by anyone on the other team who is "fresher" out of the garden than they are—that is, anyone who entered the tag zone after they did.

The following tag games are listed in the order of difficulty. I recommend that children master the skills in one game before moving on to the next.

PARTNER TAG
ISLAND TAG
TOILET TAG
UNDER THE BRIDGE
COMPOST HEAD
CAPTURE THE FLAG

Description of game:

This high-energy tag game, played in teams, uses the compost heap as a metaphor.

Most suitable for:

2nd through 4th graders

Requirements:

- 10–25 minutes
- Any indoor or outdoor space clear of obstacles and measuring about 30 steps by 20 steps
- 2 lengths of rope, each 20 steps long
- 8 cones

Pre-game setup:

Using the rope and cones, create the playing area as shown. *(See diagram on next page)*

4. A tagged child must go to the opposing team's compost heap and wait to be freed.

5. To free a captured teammate, a player must get to the opposing team's compost heap without being tagged and bring one child out. Rescuers must always take the child who has been in the compost heap the longest. The two must walk back to their team's garden.

6. The rescuer and rescued may not be tagged while making the trek back to their garden. To signal their safe status, the two children hold hands and walk with their other hands raised.

7. Rescued children may choose to come out of their garden into the tag zone at any time. As at the start of the game, they may tag anyone already in the tag zone and be tagged by anyone who enters the tag zone later than they did.

Helpful hints

1. Review safe tagging and tagger's choice. In this game, tagger's choice is particularly important since it can be difficult to keep track of who can tag whom.

2. Remind children that anyone who steps outside the boundaries of the playing area will be considered tagged.

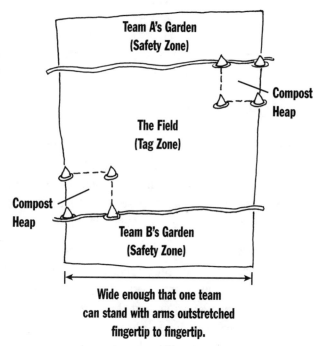

Team A's Garden
(Safety Zone)

Compost Heap

The Field
(Tag Zone)

Compost Heap

Team B's Garden
(Safety Zone)

Wide enough that one team
can stand with arms outstretched
fingertip to fingertip.

CAPTURE THE FLAG

How to play

This game often starts very slowly as children realize that initiating action could lead to capture. However, it will speed up when children begin to take risks. Because of the complexities in this game, I always introduce it after the other tag games in this series.

1. The class forms two teams, each having a jail and a flag. On each team, one child is chosen to guard the flag and another to guard the jail. These children must stand at least three steps away from the areas they are guarding. All other players line up at the rope, facing the other team.

The following tag games are listed in the order of difficulty. I recommend that children master the skills in one game before moving on to the next.

PARTNER TAG
ISLAND TAG
TOILET TAG
UNDER THE BRIDGE
COMPOST HEAD
CAPTURE THE FLAG

Description of game:

This is the ultimate in tag games because of the various roles, strategies, and counterstrategies involved. The game is at times frenetic and at times slow and calculated.

Most suitable for:

2nd through 4th graders

Requirements:

- 10–40 minutes
- Any big outside space clear of obstacles
- A long rope
- At least 1 flag per team (scraps of fabric, beanbags, tennis balls, or anything that can be held in 1 hand)
- Enough cones to define 2 jail areas

Pre-game setup:

Set up the playing area as shown. *(See diagram on next page)*

2. The object of the game is to cross into the other team's territory, capture its flag, and bring the flag back without being tagged.

3. Anyone who crosses into the opposing team's territory may be tagged by any player on that team. Tagged players must go to the opposing team's jail area and wait to be freed.

4. To free a teammate, a player must get past the jail guard, bring the child out, and the two must walk back to their side of the field. They may not be tagged on this walk back. To signify their safe status, they hold hands and walk with their other hands raised.

Helpful hints

1. Review safe tagging and tagger's choice. Remind children that anyone who steps outside the boundaries of the playing area will be considered tagged.

2. Be aware that children can become frustrated if they have to keep being the jail or flag guard. Rotate children through these roles often.

3. Here are some variations that you might want to try after the class is comfortable with the basic game:

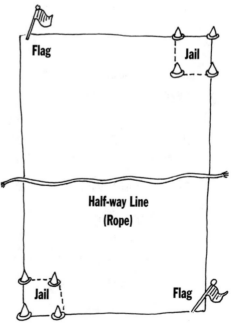

   - Have more than one flag on each side. Each team must capture all of its opponent's flags to win the game.

   - Use Frisbee discs instead of flags. Children can either run with the disc back to their own side or throw it over to their side for a teammate to catch.

   - Use a combination of flags, Frisbees, and other objects, all of which need to be captured to win the game. Because children will need to pause and think about which object to choose and how to get it back to their side, place all the objects in a safety zone at the back of each team's territory. Once in this zone, children may not be tagged. Allow only one object per child per visit to the safety zone.

RAINSTORM

How to play

This is a great activity to play when a real rainstorm is forcing you to stay indoors.

Description of game:

In this seated, follow-the-leader game, the teacher leads the class through a series of noisemaking actions that sound like a rainstorm.

Most suitable for:

Kindergartners through 4th graders

Requirements:

- 5–10 minutes
- Any indoor or outdoor space that's big enough for a seated circle
- A tape recorder (optional)

Pre-game setup:

If audiotaping the game, place the tape recorder in the middle of the circle.

1. With the teacher and students seated in a circle, the teacher makes motions and noises that sound like a rainstorm. Children imitate the teacher, continuing to make that motion/sound until the teacher changes to a different one.

2. The rainstorm motions and noises are:

   a) Raise both hands in the air with palms out, wriggle the fingers, and at the same time, make a soft whooshing noise with the mouth.

   b) Rub the palms of the hands together repeatedly.

   c) Click the fingers.

   d) Clap hands on thighs, alternating the left hand and right hand.

e) Clap hands on floor or, if playing outside, stomp feet.

f) Loudly clap hands together.

3. A storm that builds from soft to hard rain to thunder and lightning and back again will take the pattern a→b→c→d→e→f→e→d→c→b→a.

Helpful hints

1. In an alternate version of this game, the teacher begins a rainstorm motion, then passes that motion by turning to the person immediately to the left and making eye contact. That person passes the motion to the left and so on around the room. When the motion reaches the teacher, s/he begins to pass the next motion. Each student continues to make the old motion until a neighbor passes along a new one.

2. With both versions, it's important to demonstrate and practice the motions and noises before beginning the game.

3. You can choose to vary the sequence of motions and noises.

4. Some teachers tape the game so that children can hear the "rainstorm" later.

ELLA-BELLA

Description of game:

This is a moderately active guessing game that uses a ball.

Most suitable for:

1st through 4th graders

Requirements:

- 10–25 minutes
- Any indoor or outdoor space
- A tennis ball or other ball of similar size

Pre-game setup:

None

How to play

1. Children stand in a loosely formed line.

2. The teacher chooses one volunteer to be the first ball thrower. This student takes the ball, walks about ten paces away from the front of the group, and stands with his/her back to the group.

3. Without looking, the ball thrower tosses the ball back towards the group. S/he continues to stand facing away from the group.

4. Children stand in their places until the ball stops rolling. The child nearest to the ball picks it up and holds it with both hands behind her/his back.

5. The rest of the children in the group also put their hands behind their backs as though they were holding a ball.

6. The group chants: "Ella-bella, Ella-bella, who's got the ball?"

7. The ball thrower turns around and tries to guess who is holding the ball.

8. If the guess is successful, the thrower gets to throw the ball again. If the guess is unsuccessful, the child who was incorrectly named becomes the ball thrower.

Helpful hints

1. Although children initially may think the goal of this game is to grab the ball, in fact the goal is to stump the thrower so s/he can't guess who has the ball. Remind children that if they're noisy or if they fight over the ball, they'll give the thrower too many clues.

2. Having the child who is incorrectly named (i.e. not holding the ball) become the next ball thrower also takes the emphasis off grabbing the ball.

3. With older students, you can make the game more interesting by allowing the thrower to ask two or three individuals one "yes" or "no" question each. For example:

   "Julie, is the person with the ball to your right?"

   "Gerry, is the person with the ball a girl?"

   "Oisin, is the person with the ball wearing a sweater?"

GUARD DOG

BEWARE OF THE DOG

How to play

1. The teacher chooses a student to be the guard dog then blindfolds the student and leads her/him to the chair in the center of the circle.

2. The goal for the rest of the class is to retrieve the objects from under the guard dog's chair without being detected.

3. Because hearing a sound is the only way the guard dog can detect when someone attempts to retrieve an object, everyone needs to be totally silent during the game.

Description of game:

This is a quiet but active game in which objects are placed under a chair that is guarded by a blindfolded child (the guard dog). Other children must silently approach the chair and try to remove an object without being detected by the guard dog.

Most suitable for:

Kindergartners through 4th graders

Requirements:

- 5–15 minutes
- Any indoor or outdoor space big enough for a seated circle
- A chair
- A blindfold
- Several noisy objects, such as keys or a bell, to place under the chair

Pre-game setup:

- Place a chair in the middle of the space.
- Arrange the group in a circle around the chair. The larger the circle, the greater the challenge will be for those trying to get the objects.
- Place the objects under the chair.

4. The teacher points or uses some other silent gesture to let individual students know when to attempt retrieval.

5. When the guard dog hears someone attempting to retrieve an object, s/he will "bark" and point.

6. If the guard dog successfully points at an approaching or retreating player, the player is caught and must put the object back and return to the circle. The teacher decides whether the guard dog caught the player or not.

7. If a player retrieves an object and returns undetected to the circle, s/he remains seated until the game is completed.

Helpful hints

1. Before beginning the game, it's a good idea for you and the children to agree on hand signals you will use to indicate the following:

   - It's your turn to try to retrieve an object.

   - The guard dog has caught you; return to your seat.

   - The guard dog didn't catch you; you may continue.

2. Explain that the guard dog cannot point randomly, hoping to catch someone, but must point clearly and directly. Have children practice clear and direct pointing.

3. You can choose to have several children approach the chair at the same time. The number of objects under the chair and the number of children approaching should be the same so that the game doesn't become a competition over who can get to the chair first.

4. Choose a new guard dog frequently, perhaps putting a new child in the role after some, but not all, of the objects have been collected.

ONE AROUND TWO

How to play

This is a great game to build up group energy and get the blood flowing, the brain cells firing, and the smiles beaming. It can be used as a warm-up for another activity.

1. Children stand with a partner in a circle, allowing plenty of elbow room. Partners stand one in front of the other, and both children face the center of the circle.

2. Partners in the outside circle are ones; partners in the inside circle are twos.

3. At the teacher's direction, children move over, under, and around their partner. For example:

Description of game:

In this highly energetic, whole-body game, children follow directions as quickly as they can, moving over, under, and around partners.

Most suitable for:

2nd through 4th graders

Requirements:

- 5–10 minutes
- Any indoor or outdoor space, clear of obstacles and big enough for children to form a circle and move around freely. (A carpeted floor or soft grass is ideal.)

Pre-game setup:

None

Direction	Description
One *around* two…	Ones run in a tight circle around twos.
One *under* two…	Ones crawl between the legs of standing twos.
One *over* two…	Ones leap-frog over crouching twos.
One *around the outside*…	Ones run clockwise around the outside of the circle then return to their starting spot.

(Twos can also move around, over, and under ones in all these ways.)

Helpful hints

1. Before playing the game, talk with children about how to do these movements safely and then have them practice.

2. Ask for a show of hands to be sure students remember who in each pair is one and who is two.

3. Stand inside the circle and move around as you give the commands. It's OK if the circle loses some of its shape, but you should be able to see all participants so you can be sure they are moving safely.

4. Once you have gone through each command a few times, you can begin to call them out faster and faster. You can also repeat the same command several times in a row, at increasing speed.

5. To increase excitement and laughter, add vocalizations to the movements, using your own and your students' creative ideas. Here are some suggestions:

   - When they move *under*, they can make a noise like a train coming through a tunnel.

   - When they leap-frog *over*, they can make a loud "Wheeeee...."

   - When they move *around their partner*, they can make a noise like a car speeding around a race track.

   - When they move *around the outside*, they can make a noise like a police car.

SHIP

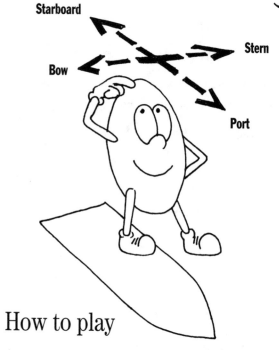

Starboard

Stern

Bow

Port

How to play

1. The class pretends that the playing area is a ship and that the teacher is the captain. Different areas of a ship have specific names:

   - *Bow* means forward end of the ship.

   - *Stern* means back end of the ship.

   - *Port* means left side of the ship.

   - *Starboard* means right side of the ship.

2. The teacher identifies these different locations within the playing area.

3. When the teacher, as captain, directs the "sailors" to different areas of their ship by calling out and pointing, students race to that location.

Description of game:

This is a running game that is fast-paced, active, and noisy.

Most suitable for:

Kindergartners through 4th graders

Requirements:

- 10–15 minutes
- An indoor or outdoor area big enough to allow children to move around energetically
- Enough rope and/or cones to mark out the boundary of a ship

Pre-game setup:

None

Helpful hints

1. The teacher can give some of the slower and younger children an advantage by calling out a command before the last child reaches the previous destination. For example, the teacher might call "bow." Just before the entire group reaches the bow, the teacher calls "stern," and everyone must run in the opposite direction. This way the slower children will have a head start.

2. This is a good game for the beginning of the school year because it's easy to learn and there are no winners or losers.

3. If you ask the children to help decide on and mark the boundaries of the "ship," using the cones and rope, they will have a clearer understanding of where the different locations are.

4. If your class has a name, you can increase the fun by naming the ship after the class. Then you can say, "As captain of the good ship (class name), I direct you to the bow."

5. When the children are responding well to the instructions, increase the challenge by reversing the direction of the ship. You can also increase the challenge by only calling out the instruction but not pointing.

Just because you join in as a player, doesn't mean you give up control of the game. It means dividing your attention between playing and observing. For example: You use peripheral vision while running to tag someone, always mindful of what every child is doing.

FROZEN TAG

How to play

This tag game requires creativity and physical flexibility more than speed. It also calls on children to take a risk to help others.

Description of game:

This is a slow-paced tag game in which players move around the playing area while balancing a beanbag on their heads. Without touching the players, the tagger tries to get them to drop the beanbag. Players can help other players retrieve a dropped beanbag.

Most suitable for:

Kindergartners through 4th graders

Requirements:

- 10–25 minutes
- An indoor or outdoor space that measures approximately 30 steps by 20 steps
- 1 beanbag for each child

Pre-game setup:

None

1. Players move about the playing area with beanbags balanced on top of their heads. If the beanbag falls off a player's head, that player is frozen in the position they're in when the beanbag falls.

2. The tagger tries to freeze players by asking them to do an action that might make the beanbags fall. The player must obey. For example, if the tagger says, "Paula, touch your toes," then Paula must try to touch her toes. If the player successfully does the action without the beanbag falling off, then the tagger moves on to someone else.

3. The tagger is not allowed to touch the players. The tagger also cannot ask the player to do cartwheels, somersaults, flips, or any other actions that can only be done by tipping the head.

4. A player who is still balancing a beanbag can retrieve a frozen player's fallen beanbag and replace it on that person's head. If a helper's beanbag falls in the attempt to help a frozen player, then the helper is also frozen.

5. Frozen players cannot help others.

6. The only time players can touch a beanbag is when they are retrieving a frozen player's bag. The tagger cannot request an action from someone who is helping a frozen player.

Helpful hints

1. Kids love to throw, squeeze, and catch beanbags, so if you want their full attention, wait until you've explained the game before handing out the beanbags.

2. Before beginning the game, have the children practice walking with beanbags on their heads. Younger students might also brainstorm and then practice how to do certain kinds of movements without letting the beanbags fall.

3. Encourage children to look for opportunities to help others.

Often in a tag game, certain tagged children wait endlessly to be freed. You can step into the game to free the children yourself. But also address this problem more fully by explaining to the group that it's everyone's job to free any tagged player.

THE PARTY GAME

Description of game:

In this quiet guessing game—often punctuated by giggles and the occasional "aha!"—children try to find a hidden pattern in words that players are saying.

Most suitable for:

3rd and 4th graders

Requirements:

- 5 minutes
- Any indoor or outdoor space large enough for a seated circle

Pre-game setup:

None

How to play

1. The teacher and children sit in a circle.

2. The teacher thinks of a rule, such as words with one syllable, words that rhyme, or words that end in *-ing*. Without telling children what the rule is, the teacher says, "I'm going to a party and I'm bringing a _____," inserting a word that fits the rule. For example, if the rule is one-syllable words, the teacher might say "I'm going to a party and I'm bringing a chair."

3. Going around the circle, each child then tries to guess what the rule is by saying "I'm going to the party and I'm bringing a _____," filling in the blank with a word that s/he thinks might fit the rule. The word does not have to be something that one would typically bring to a party. For example, if the rule is words that begin with *ch,* a child might decide to bring a "chimney."

4. If the word does fit the rule, the teacher says, "Fine." If it doesn't, the teacher says, "You'll have to think of something else to bring." Then the next child fills in the blank. As the teacher responds yea or nay to more and more guesses, students will begin to see a pattern.

Helpful hints

1. Because making guesses on demand represents a considerable risk for some children, you may want to save this game until a couple of months into the school year, when children have developed some sense of trust. Even then, remind students of caring behavior: "In this game, everyone will be making guesses, and sometimes our guesses won't be right. What can we do to make it fun and safe for everyone?"

2. The goal is not to be the first to guess correctly, but to keep the game going and help everyone "come to the party" with an appropriate object. Remind children that when they think they know the rule, they simply say the sentence with an appropriate word rather than blurting out the rule.

3. You can use this game to reinforce academic skills. For example, if you're doing a unit on water, your rule can be "things that contain water." If you're doing a spelling lesson on suffixes, the rule could be "words that end in -tion." Don't make the rule too hard to guess, though, as children can get easily frustrated.

4. Once children are familiar with the game, you may want to let students take turns as the game leader (the one who thinks up the rules).

5. Be on the lookout for children who are getting overly frustrated or embarrassed because they can't guess the rule. Ask for a big, loud group guess and end the game before it gets to this point.

ALL TiED UP

Description of game:

In this cooperative game, played in small groups, children grab each other's hands in a random pattern and then try to untangle themselves without letting go of the hands.

Most suitable for:

2nd through 4th graders

Requirements:

- 5–10 minutes
- Any indoor or outdoor space big enough to make tight circles of 6–8 people

Pre-game setup:

None

How to play

1. Children are divided into groups of six to eight.

2. Each small group stands in a tight circle with shoulders touching.

3. Group members put their hands into the center of the circle and "mix them up," so that hands are over, under, and between other hands.

4. Each person takes the hands of others in the group, one hand held by one hand. Children should not take the hand of a person standing next to them or take both hands of the same person.

5. Group members try to untangle themselves without letting go of any hands. If successful, everyone should be holding hands and there shouldn't be any crossed arms.

Helpful hints

1. Before you begin the game, use one of the groups to demonstrate how to play. It's important to take time during the demonstration to address any potential problems or questions.

2. Trying to get untangled and having fun in the process is what's important in this game. If students seem to be getting frustrated, stop the game and ask them to share strategies that could work.

3. Once the children become comfortable with this game, you can carefully set challenges. For example, you can ask the children to play the game without speaking.

4. It's best to play this game with a group that's been together for a few months since a lot depends on their ability to cooperate with each other.

When you play games with students, they see you on a different level. You forge bonds with them that endure. I've forgotten the names of most of my elementary school teachers. But I remember Ms. Quigley, my first grade teacher. She played Hopscotch with us during recess.

EXCUSE ME, PLEASE

How to play

1. The game begins with one or two taggers. As the game proceeds, children who get tagged become taggers and the original taggers become players.

2. The new tagger needs to count to five loudly before trying to tag anyone else.

3. The markers are safety bases. A child touching the safety base can't be tagged.

4. A child can only keep touching the safety base until another child comes up and says, "Excuse me, please." At that point, the first child needs to leave and start running to elude the taggers or go to a different safety base.

Description of game:

In this active tag game, the twist is that in order to enter an already occupied safety zone, children need to politely say, "Excuse me, please."

Most suitable for:

Kindergartners through 4th graders

Requirements:

- 5–15 minutes
- Any large indoor or outdoor space, clear of obstacles
- Cones, discs, or sheets of newspaper to mark safety bases, approximately one marker for every 3–4 children

Pre-game setup:

Lay out markers in a random pattern, being sure to establish clear boundaries.

Helpful hints

1. Before the game, review safe tagging and tagger's choice. Remind children that anyone who steps outside the boundaries of the playing area will be considered tagged.

2. Be sure to talk with children about how to say, "Excuse me, please." For instance, the inclination of some children might be to say the polite words in a rude or aggressive tone of voice or to say the polite words but act aggressively. Make rules about how the children should speak and act when they want to enter a safety zone and then practice this before beginning the game.

KICK THE CAN

How to play

Description of game:

This is a high-energy game with elements of Hide-and-Seek. Players come out of hiding to try and kick a can before the seeker catches them.

Most suitable for:

1st through 4th graders

Requirements:

- 5–25 minutes
- Any indoor or outdoor space big enough for students to run around energetically, with good hiding spaces available
- A can
- 4 cones that can be used to define a "jail"

Pre-game setup:

Place the can in the middle of the playing area and define a jail area.

1. The teacher chooses a seeker who stands in the middle of the circle, approximately ten paces away from the can. While the seeker counts to twenty, the rest of the children hide.

2. The object of the game is for players to come out from their hiding places and kick the can without being seen and named by the seeker. Several players can emerge at the same time.

3. When the seeker spots a player who is running to kick the can, the seeker needs to say the player's name, followed by 1, 2, 3 (for example, "Gavin, 1, 2, 3").

4. Anyone who is caught by the seeker needs to go to jail.

5. If a player manages to kick the can before the seeker says the player's name and counts to three, all those in jail are free and a new game begins with a new seeker.

Helpful hints

1. Remind students that the seeker needs to say the student's name and count to three before a player is out. You can ask students to practice the sequence of name plus 1, 2, 3 before the game begins.

2. In a variation of the game, seekers can also try to spot players in their hiding places. In that case they'd say, "I see (student's name) behind the tree, 1, 2, 3."

3. Players will quickly learn that they can work together. For example, one student might distract the seeker while another kicks the can.

4. One strategy is for several players to come out of hiding as a clump and rush towards the can together. To send them to jail, the seeker needs to say each name and follow the sequence with 1, 2, 3 before any of the players kicks the can: "Liam, Judy, Aine, 1, 2, 3." One player is likely to reach the can before the seeker can say all the names.

BALLOON RACE

Description of game:

This fast-paced relay race relies on creative cooperation between partners.

Most suitable for:

2nd through 4th graders

Requirements:

- 10–25 minutes
- Any indoor or outdoor space big enough for a "race course"
- Several balloons or slightly deflated balls

Pre-game setup:

None

How to play

1. The class divides into teams, with each team having an even number of people, if possible.

2. Each member of the team finds a partner.

3. Partners transport the balloon through the course with both people in contact with the balloon at all times. However, partners may not touch the balloon with their hands and they may not deliberately break the balloon.

4. At the end of the course, partners transfer the balloon to the next set of partners, again without touching it with their hands.

Helpful hints

1. Balloons are less likely to break if they're a little less than fully inflated. You can have a discussion with the students about what should happen if a balloon does break accidentally. Be sure you have extra balloons available for replacements.

2. Before the game begins, give students time to plan with their partners a strategy for running the course.

3. Students can be creative in figuring out how to pass the balloon from one pair of players to another. There is no wrong way to do this as long as the balloon doesn't touch the floor and the players don't touch the balloon with their hands.

4. In a traditional relay race, the first team to have all players cross the finish line without breaking any rules is the winner. However, you can vary this:

   - Declare winners based on which team showed the best cooperation.

   - Declare winners based on which team showed the most creativity.

Two things to remember when you join in as a player in a game: It's OK to win (but not all the time), and it's OK to lose (but not all the time).

ELEPHANT, PALM TREE, BOAT

How to play

1. The group sits in a circle. The teacher points to a student and says his or her name, immediately followed by the name of one of three objects. For example: "Breffni, elephant." This student and the student immediately to the right and to the left stand. The three students then pantomime the named object, using specific movements:

   - *Elephant*—The center person joins both arms together, points them downward, and sways them from side to side to mimic a trunk. The two people on either side make half-circles with their arms to mimic ears.

   - *Palm tree*—The center person raises both arms high in the air and sways them to mimic wind-blown fronds. The other two people hold their arms out to the side and sway them like a hula dancer.

- *Boat*—The center person stands on one leg, covers one eye with a hand to pretend to be a pirate, and salutes with the other hand. The people on either side paddle the boat.

2. When the trio has successfully pantomimed the object, the teacher points to another student: "Shona, boat." Shona then becomes the middle person of the next trio, who will pantomime a boat.

Helpful hints

1. Since children will need to learn and remember nine new movements, it's important to practice the movements with them before starting the game. With a young class, you might want to begin the game with only one object.

2. You can ask the children to suggest new objects or creative movements for depicting them. This allows children to feel ownership of the game.

3. Younger children might forget that the trio consists of the named child plus the child to his/her immediate right and left and that only the group of three stands to do a movement. To help them remember, practice calling the name of a student and then having the appropriate group of three stand up.

4. When you first play the game, go slowly, allowing plenty of time for the children to make the shapes. As the game progresses, you can pick up the pace.

NO-LOOK COUNTDOWN

How to play

1. Working in groups of ten, children try to count to ten with each child saying one number.

2. The rules are that:

   - Only one child can speak at a time.

   - Children can't indicate in any way (pointing, looking, nodding, etc.) who is going to say the next number.

   - Groups can't plan a strategy in advance.

   - Players can't simply go around in a circle, each saying a number in sequence.

Description of game:

This is a fun, quick game to use in an extra few minutes.

Most suitable for:

1st through 4th graders

Requirements:

- 5 minutes
- Children must be able to count to 10 and, for a variation, backwards from 10 to 1

Pre-game setup:

None

Helpful hints

1. If you have a small class, you can work with fewer than ten children in a group. If this makes the game too easy, have the class play as one large group.

2. It's important to keep this game fast and light. If a group makes a mistake, have them quickly start over until they get to ten. If groups seem to get frustrated, either mix up the groups and try again or save the game for another day.

ABOUT THE AUTHOR

Adrian Harrison grew up in Dundalk, Ireland. He moved from Ireland to Canada in 1988 to attend the University of Prince Edward Island, receiving his BA in 1992. He returned to Ireland, where he attended the University of Limerick and taught for several years. He moved to the United States in 1999.

Adrian has worked with children as both coach and teacher since 1986. In Ireland, he taught physical education at the elementary and secondary level. In the United States, he taught fifth, seventh, and eighth grades as well as physical education at Greenfield Center School, the independent K–8 school founded by Northeast Foundation for Children.

Adrian is an internationally certified soccer coach known for his innovative, fun-based coaching style. In addition to teaching and coaching, Adrian is a talented artist, creating artwork in styles ranging from portraits to cartoons.